PRIMOŽ ROGLIC BIOGRAPHY

The Dynamics of Speed and Strategy in Competitive Cycling — A Champion's Journey from Slovenia to Stardom

GEORGE F. JONES

All rights reserved.

No part of this publication may be reproduced, distributed, or transmitted in any form or by any means, including photocopying, recording, or other electronic or mechanical methods, without the prior written permission of the publisher, except in the case of brief quotations embodied in critical reviews and certain other noncommercial uses permitted by copyright law.

Copyright © George F. Jones, 2024

Disclaimer

This book contains information that is solely meant to be educational. Despite their best efforts to present accurate and current information, the author and publisher disclaim all expressed and implied representations and warranties regarding the availability, completeness, accuracy, reliability, suitability, or suitability of the content contained herein for any purpose. The publisher and the author disclaim all responsibility for any loss or harm, including without limitation, consequential or indirect loss or damage, or any loss or damage at all resulting from lost profits or data resulting from using this book.

TABLE OF CONTENTS

INTRODUCTION
CHAPTER 1: EARLY LIFE AND BACKGROUND
CHAPTER 2: THE ROAD TO PROFESSIONAL CYCLING
CHAPTER 3: RISE THROUGH THE RANKS
CHAPTER 4: MASTERING THE ART OF TIME TRIALS
CHAPTER 5: GRAND TOURS AND MAJOR VICTORIES
CHAPTER 6: OVERCOMING ADVERSITY
CHAPTER 7: THE ROLE OF TECHNOLOGY IN TRAINING
CHAPTER 8: LIFE BEYOND THE BIKE
CHAPTER 9: LEGACY AND IMPACT ON THE SPORT
CONCLUSION

INTRODUCTION

In the thrilling final kilometers of a high-stakes mountain stage, with the crowd roaring and the tension palpable, Primož Roglič surged ahead. The air was electric, every pedal stroke measured yet fierce, as the Slovenian cyclist closed in on victory. Millions of fans worldwide watched in awe as he attacked the summit, his focus unwavering despite the fatigue etched across his face. It was moments like these—tense, dramatic, and extraordinary—that defined Roglič's rise to cycling superstardom. With the finish line in sight, Roglič powered through, not just winning the stage but also solidifying his reputation as one of the most resilient and strategic riders in modern cycling. His victory was not merely about the race itself, but about the journey that had brought him there—a journey of remarkable determination, adaptation, and sheer willpower.

For cycling fans, these moments encapsulate the essence of what makes Primož Roglič one of the sport's most compelling figures. But to truly understand the depth of his impact, one must look beyond the races and results. This book is not just a recounting of victories and podium finishes; it's an exploration of heart, perseverance, and the strategic brilliance that has come to define Roglič's career.

Before Roglič became a household name in professional cycling, known for his exceptional time trials and dominance in

Grand Tours, he was a ski jumper from a small town in Slovenia with no clear path to cycling fame. Raised in a country where winter sports reign supreme, Roglič's journey to the pinnacle of competitive cycling was anything but conventional. He didn't follow the typical path of a childhood spent on bikes or in junior cycling leagues. Instead, Roglič was a latecomer to the sport, switching from ski jumping to cycling after a devastating fall that nearly ended his athletic career. It was a decision that would change his life forever, leading him to the world stage of one of the most grueling and demanding sports in existence.

In his early years, Roglič faced skepticism and doubt. A ski jumper turning to cycling? The odds seemed stacked against him. Yet,

Roglič embraced every challenge, transforming himself into a versatile and powerful cyclist. His ability to adapt—both to the demands of the sport and the unpredictable conditions of races—became his greatest strength. Whether conquering brutal mountain climbs, mastering technical time trials, or navigating the tactical complexities of the peloton, Roglič's versatility set him apart in a sport where specialization often dominates.

Roglič's rise was not solely about his physical abilities, though they were undeniable. His mental fortitude, sharp racing instincts, and strategic acumen quickly became his hallmarks. In a sport where one bad decision or misjudged moment can spell disaster, Roglič developed a reputation for his cool-headedness under pressure. He wasn't just a rider who could win races—he was a rider who could outthink his opponents, leveraging every bit of his experience and knowledge to gain an edge. His ability to read the race, anticipate attacks, and execute perfectly-timed moves transformed him into one of cycling's most formidable competitors.

But it wasn't just Roglič's performances that endeared him to fans across the world. His humility, work ethic, and grounded nature made him a beloved figure not just in Slovenia, but in the global cycling community. Despite his remarkable success, Roglič has remained deeply connected to his roots, never forgetting the challenges he faced on his unconventional path to the top. He has become a symbol of resilience—proof that setbacks can be launching pads for greatness, and that perseverance can carry you further than talent alone.

As Roglič's career progressed, his tactical brilliance and mental toughness came into sharper focus, particularly in high-pressure races like the Tour de France and the Vuelta a España. These events are grueling, multi-week tests of endurance, strategy, and sheer willpower, and Roglič's ability to perform at his best under the most intense conditions has made him a staple of the podium. Time and again, when the stakes were highest, Roglič delivered, showcasing not just his physical prowess but also his unmatched ability to strategize in the heat of competition.

His victories in Grand Tours—along with his heroic efforts in races like the Olympic Games—have cemented Roglič's place among the all-time greats of the sport. But his legacy is about more than titles and accolades. Roglič has redefined what it means to be a champion in the modern era of cycling, blending old-school toughness with cutting-edge tactics and a deep respect for the sport's traditions.

This biography explores more than just the races Roglič has won—it tells the story of his evolution as an athlete, his ability to adapt and excel in one of the world's most challenging sports, and his journey from Slovenia to global stardom. It's a celebration of a cyclist who has redefined the sport with his speed, strategy, and tenacity. From his humble beginnings to his unforgettable moments in the world's biggest races, Primož Roglič's story is one that will inspire readers and cyclists alike, serving as a testament to the power of determination, adaptability, and never giving up on your dreams.

CHAPTER 1: EARLY LIFE AND BACKGROUND

Growing Up in Slovenia

Primož Roglič was born on October 29, 1989, in the small town of Škofja Loka, located in Slovenia. This quaint town is surrounded by mountains and forests, offering a beautiful backdrop for a childhood filled with outdoor activities. Growing up in a tight-knit community, Roglič was immersed in the rich culture and history of Slovenia from an early age. The country is known for its stunning landscapes, including lakes, rivers, and hills, which would later play a significant role in shaping his athletic career.

In this environment, family played a crucial role in shaping Roglič's early life. He was raised in a household that valued hard work and determination. His parents instilled a sense of discipline and perseverance in him, traits that would become essential in his later pursuits as a professional athlete. His father worked in construction, while his mother was a nurse, providing a balanced upbringing that emphasized both physical labor and care for others.

As a child, Roglič was naturally curious and energetic. He spent much of his time playing outside, exploring the beautiful surroundings of his hometown. The mountains offered plenty of opportunities for adventure, from hiking to skiing in the winter months. This connection to nature would have a lasting impact on him, as he learned to appreciate the beauty of his homeland while developing an adventurous spirit.

Roglič's childhood was not without its challenges. Like many children, he faced the ups and downs of growing up, including the pressure to perform well in school and the desire to fit in with his peers. However, his natural athleticism shone through early on, and he quickly developed a passion for sports. He participated in various activities, including soccer and skiing, which laid the foundation for his future success in competitive sports.

Skiing became a significant part of Roglič's life during his formative years. The winter sports culture in Slovenia is strong, with many children introduced to skiing at a young age. Roglič took to the slopes, spending weekends and holidays honing his skills. He became quite skilled at ski jumping, a popular discipline in Slovenia, and even competed at a national level. This early success in skiing not only boosted his confidence but also taught him the importance of dedication and discipline in pursuing one's dreams.

Despite his early achievements in ski jumping, Roglič faced a turning point that would alter the course of his life. A serious injury during a competition sidelined him for an extended period, forcing him to reconsider his future in the sport. While recovering, he spent time reflecting on his passions and goals. It was during this period of introspection that he began to explore other athletic avenues, ultimately leading him to cycling.

Growing up in Slovenia, Roglič was also influenced by the country's rich sports history. Slovenia has produced numerous world-class athletes across various disciplines, from basketball to skiing. The success of these athletes served as inspiration for Roglič, instilling in him the belief that greatness was attainable with hard work and dedication. This belief would become a driving force in his life, motivating him to push beyond his limits and strive for excellence in whatever sport he chose to pursue.

Early Athletic Influences

Primož Roglič's athletic journey began long before he became a household name in cycling. His early influences shaped not only his physical abilities but also his mental approach to sports. Growing up in Slovenia, a country with a rich sporting culture, he was exposed to various athletic pursuits from a young age. This exposure played a pivotal role in his development as an athlete.

As a child, Roglič participated in multiple sports, with soccer being one of the most popular in his community. Like many boys his age, he played soccer with his friends after school, enjoying the camaraderie and competition. These games taught him essential skills such as teamwork, strategy, and the thrill of competition. While soccer was fun, it was skiing that captured his heart, providing a perfect blend of excitement and challenge.

Skiing became a central part of Roglič's identity during his formative years. His family often took trips to the mountains during the winter months, allowing him to immerse himself in the sport. Skiing not only honed his physical abilities but also instilled a sense of discipline and focus. The demanding nature of the sport requires athletes to maintain a rigorous training regimen, and Roglič embraced this challenge wholeheartedly.

He initially found his niche in ski jumping, where he showcased remarkable talent. The rush of soaring through the air appealed to his adventurous spirit, and he quickly rose through the ranks in the sport.

Competing in ski jumping events provided him with valuable lessons in resilience. The highs of success and the lows of failure taught him that sports are often unpredictable and that perseverance is essential.

Roglič's success in ski jumping was partly due to his influences outside of his immediate family. Slovenia boasts a proud history of winter sports, with several prominent ski jumpers and skiers who served as role models for young athletes. Watching these athletes compete and achieve greatness ignited a fire within him. Their determination and passion for the sport inspired him to push himself harder and dream bigger. He idolized figures like Primož Peterka, a renowned ski jumper who had achieved international success, and he aspired to follow in their footsteps.

In addition to the local influences, Roglič's athletic journey was shaped by the broader sporting community in Slovenia. The country has a deep appreciation for sports, with various clubs and organizations dedicated to nurturing young talent. These institutions provided young athletes like Roglič with opportunities to train, compete, and learn from experienced coaches. He participated in youth training camps, where he developed his skills alongside other aspiring athletes, fostering a sense of camaraderie and healthy competition.

However, his journey took an unexpected turn due to an injury that sidelined him from ski jumping. While this setback could have deterred many young athletes, Roglič viewed it as a moment of reflection. He realized that he had to adapt and explore new avenues for his athletic ambitions. During this period, he discovered cycling, which would ultimately become his true calling.

The transition from ski jumping to cycling was not as simple as it might seem. It required a shift in mindset and training. While both sports demanded physical endurance, the techniques and strategies varied significantly. Roglič approached cycling with the same determination that had characterized his skiing career. He immersed himself in the world of cycling, studying the techniques, training regimens, and tactics employed by successful cyclists.

As he began to train for cycling, Roglič drew on the lessons learned from his earlier experiences in skiing. The discipline, focus, and competitive spirit he developed as a ski jumper helped him adapt to the demands of cycling. He utilized his background in endurance sports to build stamina, pushing himself through grueling training sessions. While he initially pursued ski jumping, the lessons learned during that time would serve him well when he transitioned to cycling, setting the stage for a remarkable career ahead.

Discovering Cycling

Primož Roglič's journey into the world of cycling was a transformative experience, marking a significant turning point in his athletic career. Following an injury that forced him to step away from ski jumping, Roglič found himself at a crossroads. Instead of allowing this setback to define him, he took it as an opportunity to explore a different sport that would ultimately lead him to greatness.

During his recovery, Roglič sought ways to stay active and maintain his fitness levels. He had always enjoyed the thrill of competition, and cycling became an appealing option. Slovenia's scenic landscapes, with its winding roads and beautiful countryside, provided the perfect setting for him to explore this new passion. He began cycling recreationally, riding through the picturesque valleys and mountains that surrounded his hometown.

Initially, cycling was a means to stay fit, but it quickly transformed into a passion. Roglič was captivated by the freedom and exhilaration that came with riding on two wheels. The physical demands of cycling were similar to those of ski jumping, requiring stamina, strength, and focus. He realized that many of the skills he had developed as a ski jumper could be applied to cycling, making the transition smoother than expected.

As he became more serious about cycling, Roglič sought guidance from local coaches and joined a cycling club in his community. This step introduced him to a structured training environment, where he could learn the nuances of the sport and refine his skills. The club provided him with valuable resources, including access to experienced cyclists who offered mentorship and support.

Through the cycling club, Roglič began participating in local races, which further fueled his desire to compete. His competitive spirit shone through, and he quickly gained recognition for his talent. His background in ski jumping gave him a unique edge, as he possessed the physical conditioning and mental toughness necessary for cycling. He tackled the hills with confidence and approached races with the determination to succeed.

One of the pivotal moments in Roglič's cycling journey came when he participated in a regional competition. This race served as a proving ground, allowing him to showcase his skills against other emerging cyclists. Despite being relatively new to the sport, Roglič finished impressively, earning the respect of fellow competitors and coaches alike. This early success solidified his decision to pursue cycling seriously.

As Roglič continued to improve, he began to understand the intricacies of competitive cycling. He learned about the importance of strategy, teamwork, and pacing in races. Unlike ski jumping, where individual performance was paramount, cycling required collaboration with teammates to achieve success. Roglič embraced this aspect of the sport, recognizing that working together could lead to greater achievements.

His passion for cycling soon caught the attention of scouts from larger cycling teams. As he honed his skills, he received opportunities to compete at higher levels, including national and international races. This was a dream come true for Roglič, who had once been a young athlete navigating the world of sports in a small town. He now found himself on the cusp of a professional cycling career, ready to make his mark.

Despite the excitement of these opportunities, Roglič remained grounded. He understood that the path to success would require hard work, dedication, and resilience. He embraced the challenges that lay ahead, focusing on improving his performance and learning from each race. The lessons learned from ski jumping about mental toughness and perseverance became invaluable as he faced the rigors of competitive cycling.

As Roglič went deeper into the cycling world, he also connected with fellow cyclists who shared his passion. These relationships formed a supportive network, allowing him to learn from their experiences and gain insights into the sport. Together, they pushed each other to achieve their goals, fostering a sense of camaraderie that would be essential in the competitive landscape of cycling.

CHAPTER 2: THE ROAD TO PROFESSIONAL CYCLING

Transitioning from Ski Jumping to Cycling

Primož Roglič's transition from ski jumping to cycling is a remarkable story of resilience and adaptation. After achieving early success in ski jumping, he faced a significant setback when an injury forced him to step back from the sport he loved. However, instead of giving up on his athletic dreams, Roglič chose to explore a new path: cycling. This decision was not only a turning point in his career but also a testament to his determination and willingness to embrace change.

Initially, the idea of switching sports seemed daunting. Ski jumping and cycling are vastly different, both in technique and approach. Ski jumping requires a unique set of skills, including the ability to launch off a ramp and glide through the air, while cycling focuses on endurance, speed, and strategy on the road. Nevertheless, Roglič found that many of the qualities he developed as a ski jumper could serve him well in cycling. The strength and balance he had honed while soaring through the air translated into powerful legs and stability on the bike.

During the early days of his transition, Roglič took to cycling as a means of rehabilitation. He began riding his bike along the scenic roads of Slovenia, finding joy in the freedom and thrill of cycling. The beautiful landscapes and varied terrain around Škofja Loka became his training ground. He rode through the hills and valleys, relishing the feeling of wind against his face and the rush of adrenaline as he navigated the winding roads. This newfound passion helped him regain his fitness and discover a love for cycling that he had not anticipated.

While cycling provided a new outlet for his athleticism, Roglič was aware that to succeed in this sport, he would need to adopt a different mindset. He spent time studying the techniques of successful cyclists and learning about the strategies involved in competitive racing. This included understanding the importance of endurance training, pacing, and teamwork, all of which played crucial roles in a cyclist's success. Roglič approached this learning process with the same dedication that he had applied to ski jumping.

One of the challenges Roglič faced was overcoming the initial doubts that came with starting a new sport. The fear of the unknown can be intimidating, especially when transitioning from a well-established career in ski jumping to the uncharted territory of cycling. However, he leaned on the lessons learned during his ski jumping career—lessons of perseverance, hard work, and the importance of setting goals. He started small, participating in local rides and gradually increasing the intensity and distance of his training sessions.

As he trained more seriously, Roglič began to notice improvements in his performance. His body adapted to the demands of cycling, and he built up the strength and endurance needed for longer rides. He also began to experiment with different cycling techniques, learning how to handle the bike effectively and navigate various terrains. The early challenges of balancing and pedaling soon became second nature to him, and he found himself enjoying the process of learning and improving.

Another key aspect of Roglič's transition was the sense of community he found within the cycling world. He connected with local cycling clubs, where he met other riders who shared his passion. This camaraderie provided a supportive environment for him to learn and grow as a cyclist. Training with others not only pushed him to improve but also helped him build friendships that would last throughout his career. The shared experiences of training, racing, and overcoming obstacles fostered a sense of belonging that further motivated him to succeed.

As Roglič's confidence grew, he began to consider the possibility of competing in cycling events. The thought of racing filled him with excitement, but it also brought a degree of apprehension. Competing would require a different level of commitment and preparation than he had experienced in ski jumping. He understood that to excel in cycling, he would need to embrace the competitive spirit and channel the same determination that had driven him in his previous sport.

Joining the Slovenian Cycling Team

As Primož Roglič settled into his new life as a cyclist, he soon realized that joining a competitive cycling team was essential for his growth and development in the sport. After transitioning from ski jumping, he had spent considerable time honing his skills, building endurance, and learning the ins and outs of cycling. Now, he needed the structure and support that a professional team could provide.

Roglič's journey to joining the Slovenian Cycling Team was not without its hurdles. As a newcomer to the sport, he was aware that he needed to prove himself to earn a place among more experienced riders. To gain the attention of the team's coaches and managers, he focused on participating in local and regional races, aiming to showcase his abilities and determination. These races provided him with invaluable experience, allowing him to learn about racing strategies, pacing, and the dynamics of group cycling.

Competing in these events was both thrilling and nerve-wracking for Roglič. He faced stiff competition from seasoned cyclists who had spent years perfecting their skills. However, he approached each race with a mindset focused on improvement rather than solely on winning. With every pedal stroke, he learned more about his strengths and weaknesses, refining his technique and developing a better understanding of how to race effectively.

Word of Roglič's talent began to spread within the cycling community. Coaches and scouts started to take notice of the young cyclist from Škofja Loka who was making waves in the local racing scene. His natural athleticism, combined with the dedication he demonstrated in training, set him apart from his peers. As he continued to impress in regional races, the prospect of joining the Slovenian Cycling Team became more realistic.

In addition to his impressive performances, Roglič's character also played a crucial role in his journey to the team. His work ethic, determination, and positive attitude made him a desirable candidate for any cycling organization. Fellow cyclists and coaches recognized his potential, often remarking on his willingness to learn and adapt. These qualities endeared him to many in the cycling community, paving the way for future opportunities.

Eventually, after a series of successful races and positive recommendations from coaches, Roglič received an invitation to join the Slovenian Cycling Team. This was a significant milestone in his career and a dream come true. Joining a professional team offered him the chance to compete at higher levels, receive expert coaching, and train alongside experienced cyclists. It marked the beginning of a new chapter in his journey as a competitive athlete.

Once he officially joined the team, Roglič was welcomed into a world filled with camaraderie, competition, and shared goals. The team environment provided him with the resources and support he needed to continue developing as a cyclist. Coaches offered tailored training programs, focusing on his strengths while addressing areas for improvement. They also provided invaluable advice on race tactics, nutrition, and mental preparation—essential components for any aspiring professional cyclist.

Training with the team was an eye-opening experience for Roglič. He quickly realized the importance of teamwork in cycling, where success often hinges on the collective efforts of the riders. The camaraderie and shared experiences fostered a sense of belonging that motivated him to push harder. He learned how to draft behind teammates to conserve energy, strategize during races, and communicate effectively while riding in a pack.

As Roglič continued to grow within the team, he was exposed to larger competitions, including national and international events. Competing at this level was both exhilarating and daunting. The atmosphere was charged with intensity, and he found himself racing alongside some of the best cyclists in the world. This exposure provided him with a greater understanding of the sport and its competitive landscape.

With each race, Roglič absorbed lessons that would shape his development as a cyclist. He observed the tactics employed by seasoned professionals, learning about pacing, positioning, and how to make split-second decisions in high-pressure situations. These experiences were invaluable, as they taught him not only about cycling but also about the mental fortitude required to compete at a high level.

First Steps in Competitive Racing

With his place secured on the Slovenian Cycling Team, Primož Roglič embarked on a journey into the world of competitive racing. This chapter of his life was filled with excitement, challenges, and invaluable lessons as he navigated the early stages of his cycling career. His first experiences in competitive racing would shape his understanding of the sport and lay the groundwork for future success.

Roglič's initial races were often regional events, where he faced fellow cyclists eager to prove themselves. These competitions offered a chance to test his skills against others who shared his passion for cycling. The atmosphere at these events was electric, filled with anticipation and camaraderie. As riders lined up at the start, the excitement in the air was palpable. Roglič embraced the thrill of competition, eager to showcase the skills he had developed during his training.

In his first few races, Roglič learned that competitive cycling is about more than just speed; it's also about strategy and teamwork. He quickly discovered that races could be unpredictable, with factors such as weather conditions, road surfaces, and the dynamics of competing cyclists all playing a role in the outcome. Each race was a unique challenge that required careful planning and adaptability.

One of the most important lessons Roglič learned early on was the significance of pacing. In cycling, maintaining a steady rhythm is crucial to avoiding fatigue and ensuring endurance throughout the race. He often found himself caught up in the adrenaline of the competition, pushing himself to keep up with the leaders. However, he quickly realized that racing is not just about sprinting ahead; it's also about knowing when to conserve energy and when to unleash his speed. This understanding would serve him well in future races.

As Roglič progressed through the ranks, he faced various obstacles that tested his determination. From challenging climbs to sudden weather changes, each race presented new hurdles. However, he embraced these challenges, viewing them as opportunities to learn and grow as a cyclist. His resilience and positive attitude became key factors in his ability to overcome adversity and continue improving.

The camaraderie among cyclists also played a significant role in Roglič's early experiences. He formed friendships with fellow riders, sharing both the highs and lows of racing. This sense of community provided a support network that helped him navigate the pressures of competition. In moments of struggle, the encouragement from teammates and peers motivated him to push through challenges and remain focused on his goals.

As he gained experience in regional races, Roglič began to develop a competitive edge. His determination and strategic mindset allowed him to excel in different types of races, whether it was a flat sprint or a challenging mountainous route. He learned to read the race dynamics, identifying when to break away from the pack and when to work collaboratively with teammates. This ability to strategize would become a hallmark of his racing style in the years to come.

Participating in his first national races was a pivotal moment for Roglič. Competing at this level exposed him to a higher caliber of athletes and a more intense competitive atmosphere. The stakes were higher, and the pressure to perform increased. However, he approached these races with confidence, knowing that his hard work and dedication had prepared him for this moment.

CHAPTER 3: RISE THROUGH THE RANKS

Early Career Highlights

As Primož Roglič settled into his role as a competitive cyclist, the early years of his career were marked by significant achievements that laid the foundation for his future success. Each race and each victory helped to shape him into the world-class cyclist he would become. From regional competitions to national titles, Roglič's journey through the ranks began to take shape, filled with moments that would define his early career.

In the beginning, Roglič participated in local and regional races, gradually increasing the level of competition. These races were not only about speed; they provided an opportunity for him to learn, adapt, and showcase his talent. One of his first significant achievements came when he won a series of local events, drawing the attention of coaches and cycling enthusiasts. His performances were impressive, and he quickly established himself as a rising star in the cycling community. This early recognition was crucial, as it motivated him to work even harder and aspire to greater heights.

One of the standout moments in Roglič's early career occurred during a national competition. He entered the race with determination, eager to prove himself against some of Slovenia's best cyclists. As the race unfolded, he demonstrated remarkable endurance and strategic thinking, positioning himself well throughout the course. In the final stretch, Roglič unleashed his speed, sprinting ahead of his competitors to claim victory. This win was not just a testament to his physical abilities but also showcased his mental toughness and willingness to seize the moment.

This victory was significant for Roglič. It not only solidified his place among the top cyclists in Slovenia but also provided him with the confidence to compete at higher levels. Winning a national title opened doors for him, allowing him to gain access to more prestigious races and further his career. The experience of standing on the podium, holding the winner's trophy, fueled his passion for cycling and reaffirmed his commitment to the sport.

As he continued to excel, Roglič participated in several junior competitions, where he faced tougher opponents and more challenging courses. These races were essential for his growth as a cyclist. Each event tested his skills and endurance, pushing him to improve and adapt. He learned the importance of teamwork, strategy, and the dynamics of racing in a pack. The lessons learned in these races would prove invaluable as he advanced in his career.

With every victory, Roglič gained recognition not only in Slovenia but also on the international stage. His performances caught the attention of cycling teams beyond his home country. Coaches and scouts recognized his potential and were impressed by his dedication to the sport. This interest paved the way for opportunities that would further elevate his career.

In addition to his race victories, Roglič's character and attitude played a significant role in his rise through the ranks. He was known for his humility and willingness to learn from others. This mindset allowed him to soak up knowledge from experienced cyclists and coaches, understanding that there was always room for improvement. His dedication to training and his ability to maintain a positive outlook, even in the face of challenges, made him a respected figure among his peers.

As Roglič began to compete in more prestigious events, he faced a new level of competition. Each race brought together some of the best cyclists in the world, and the challenges became greater. However, he embraced these opportunities with enthusiasm. The thrill of racing against top-tier athletes pushed him to raise his game and strive for excellence.

With each race, Roglič's skills improved, and his reputation grew. He started to earn podium finishes consistently, showcasing his talent on larger platforms. This success not only built his confidence but also opened up opportunities for sponsorships and support from cycling organizations. His early career highlights set the stage for a promising future, positioning him as one of the cyclists to watch in the coming years.

Competing in the UCI World Tour

As Primož Roglič continued to establish himself in the world of competitive cycling, the opportunity to compete in the UCI World Tour became a turning point in his career. The UCI World Tour is a series of prestigious cycling races held annually, featuring the best cyclists and teams from around the globe. It represents the pinnacle of professional cycling, and being part of this elite competition was a dream come true for Roglič.

When Roglič first received the chance to compete in the UCI World Tour, he felt a mixture of excitement and nervousness. He was eager to test his skills against some of the best cyclists in the world but also understood the level of commitment and preparation required to compete at such a high level. This was a new chapter in his career, and he was determined to make the most of the opportunity.

One of the most significant aspects of competing in the UCI World Tour was the exposure to a diverse range of races. The tour included events with various terrains and conditions, from flat sprints to challenging mountain stages. Each race presented unique challenges, testing not only physical abilities but also strategic thinking and mental fortitude. Roglič approached each event with a clear focus, studying the course and developing a plan to optimize his performance.

In his early appearances in the UCI World Tour, Roglič faced some tough competition. He raced alongside seasoned professionals who had years of experience and a wealth of knowledge about the intricacies of the sport. However, rather than feeling intimidated, Roglič embraced the challenge. He viewed each race as a learning opportunity, soaking up insights from his competitors and gaining valuable experience.

As he competed in the UCI World Tour, Roglič quickly established a reputation as a strong rider. His performances showcased his versatility and ability to adapt to different race conditions. Whether navigating the flat roads of a classic race or tackling the steep climbs of a mountain stage, he proved himself to be a formidable competitor. This adaptability became one of his defining characteristics, allowing him to excel in a variety of racing situations.

One of the highlights of Roglič's early UCI World Tour experience was his participation in the Vuelta a España, one of cycling's Grand Tours. This three-week race is known for its grueling stages and challenging courses. Competing in the Vuelta was a significant milestone for Roglič, as it offered him the chance to race against the best in the sport over a longer period.

During the Vuelta, Roglič showcased his ability to withstand the rigors of long-distance racing. His endurance and determination were evident as he tackled each stage, often finishing among the top competitors. This performance solidified his status as a rising star in professional cycling and garnered attention from fans and media alike. The experience of competing in such a prestigious event helped him grow as a cyclist, building confidence and fueling his ambition for future successes.

While competing at the UCI World Tour level, Roglič learned the importance of teamwork. Cycling is often seen as an individual sport, but success in races frequently depends on the support of teammates. Roglič quickly recognized that working together with his team could lead to better outcomes. He learned how to communicate effectively with his teammates, coordinating efforts during races to maximize their chances of success.

The camaraderie developed among team members became essential during the demanding UCI World Tour races. The challenges faced on the road fostered a sense of unity and support. Roglič and his teammates pushed each other to perform at their best, celebrating victories together and learning from setbacks. This teamwork not only improved their individual performances but also strengthened their bond as a cycling team.

As Roglič continued to compete in the UCI World Tour, his presence in the cycling community grew. His performances garnered respect from fellow cyclists and fans, and he began to attract sponsorship opportunities that would further support his career. The experiences gained through these competitions allowed him to refine his skills and develop a deeper understanding of the sport.

The Importance of Team Support

Throughout his rise in competitive cycling, Primož Roglič learned that success is rarely achieved alone. The importance of team support became increasingly evident as he navigated the challenges and triumphs of his career. From the early days of his transition from ski jumping to cycling to competing at the highest levels of the sport, the role of his teammates, coaches, and support staff was instrumental in his development as an athlete.

When Roglič first joined the Slovenian Cycling Team, he quickly recognized the value of being part of a cohesive unit. Cycling is a unique sport where individual talent must be complemented by effective teamwork. While riders often compete individually, the dynamics of racing require collaboration and support from teammates. This realization helped Roglič understand that his success would depend not only on his own efforts but also on the contributions of those around him.

Team support in cycling comes in various forms, from physical assistance during races to emotional encouragement during tough times. Teammates play a vital role in helping each other navigate the challenges of competition. For instance, during races, cyclists often take turns leading the pack, allowing teammates to draft behind and conserve energy. This strategic collaboration is essential for maintaining speed and endurance throughout the race. Roglič learned to rely on his teammates during these critical moments, recognizing that their collective efforts could lead to greater success.

Team dynamics extend beyond the races themselves. The training environment created by the team fostered camaraderie and motivation. Roglič trained alongside his teammates, pushing each other to improve and reach their full potential. The shared experiences of long rides, grueling workouts, and preparation for races helped strengthen their bond. This sense of unity created a positive atmosphere that inspired

Roglič to work harder and stay focused on his goals.

As Roglič progressed through the ranks, he became part of professional cycling teams that provided a more structured environment. The support staff, including coaches, trainers, and nutritionists, played a crucial role in his development. These professionals helped him fine-tune his training regimen, optimize his nutrition, and develop strategies for racing. Their expertise contributed to Roglič's growth as an athlete, allowing him to compete at the highest levels of the sport.

Coaches, in particular, were instrumental in guiding Roglič's development. They analyzed his performances, provided constructive feedback, and helped him identify areas for improvement. This mentorship was invaluable, as it allowed him to learn from someone with a wealth of experience in the sport. Coaches played a pivotal role in shaping his training programs and race strategies, helping him develop the skills needed to excel in competitive cycling.

In addition to physical and technical support, the emotional encouragement from teammates and coaches was equally important. Cycling can be an intense and demanding sport, both mentally and physically. The highs of victory and the lows of defeat can take a toll on a cyclist's confidence and motivation. Having a supportive team around him provided Roglič with the reassurance he needed during challenging times. The encouragement from teammates and coaches helped him stay focused, reminding him of his abilities and the hard work he had put into his training.

As Roglič gained recognition in the cycling world, the significance of team support became even more apparent. Competing at high-stakes events like the UCI World Tour required not only individual talent but also the collective strength of the team. Success in these races often depended on how well the team worked together, executing strategies and supporting one another throughout the race. Roglič learned to appreciate the importance of communication and trust within the team, understanding that their combined efforts were key to achieving their goals.

CHAPTER 4: MASTERING THE ART OF TIME TRIALS

Techniques for Success

Mastering the art of time trials in cycling requires not just physical strength but also mental sharpness and precision in technique. Unlike a typical road race where cyclists jostle for position and draft behind one another, a time trial is a solo event. In this format, every cyclist starts separately and races against the clock, making it a true test of individual ability. Success in time trials depends on a combination of pacing, equipment optimization, aerodynamics, and mental endurance.

One of the most critical techniques for time trial success is pacing. In many races, riders can afford to save energy by riding in a group and then make a late sprint to the finish. However, in time trials, every second counts from the moment the rider begins. Cyclists must pace themselves carefully to ensure they don't burn out too early. The temptation to push too hard in the opening kilometers can be strong, but a wise cyclist knows that the real challenge is maintaining a consistent speed throughout the entire race. Pacing requires both discipline and deep knowledge of one's physical limits. Cyclists often practice maintaining steady power output over long distances, monitoring their heart rate or using power meters to keep their effort in check.

Aerodynamics is another crucial factor in time trials. Cyclists spend hours perfecting their riding position to minimize wind resistance. The more aerodynamic a cyclist can be, the less energy they need to expend to maintain speed. To achieve this, riders often lower their body position, tucking their elbows and shoulders in to reduce drag. Specialized time trial bikes are also designed to optimize aerodynamics, with sleek frames, aerodynamic wheels, and gear setups that help reduce friction with the air. Even the clothing and helmets cyclists wear in a time trial are specifically designed to help them slice through the wind more efficiently.

Along with aerodynamics, the equipment a cyclist uses can make a significant difference in their performance. Time trial bikes are equipped with aero bars, allowing the rider to lean forward in a low position. This setup helps the cyclist stay in a streamlined posture, reducing air resistance. These bikes are typically lighter and more rigid than regular road bikes, making them more responsive and efficient for time trials. Tires are another important consideration. Cyclists often choose narrower, high-pressure tires with minimal tread to reduce rolling resistance and improve speed.

Mental strength plays a massive role in time trial success. Since riders are alone on the course, without the direct pressure of other competitors alongside them, the mental game becomes just as important as physical preparation. Staying focused for the entire duration of the race, especially during longer time trials, can be challenging. Cyclists need to maintain their rhythm, ignore discomfort, and push through fatigue. The isolation of the event means that there are no external cues to spur a rider on—no crowds, no direct competitors to draft behind. It's just the rider, the bike, and the clock. Those who excel at time trials are often mentally tough, able to maintain their concentration and push themselves harder even when they are struggling.

A cyclist's ability to recover during the race is another key factor. While time trials demand sustained effort, there are moments when a rider can briefly ease up, such as when descending or riding through a section of the course with a tailwind. Knowing when to back off slightly and recover a bit without losing much time is a skill that comes with experience. These brief moments of recovery can be enough to prevent the rider from hitting a wall of fatigue later in the race.

Nutrition and hydration also play a role, though they are less obvious to the casual observer. Leading up to the race, cyclists need to manage their food intake to ensure they have enough energy to perform at their peak. Eating the right balance of carbohydrates and proteins in the days before the event ensures that the muscles are fueled and ready to go. On the day of the race, cyclists are careful about how much they eat and drink to avoid feeling too full or dehydrated during the race. For longer time trials, taking quick sips of water or sports drinks during the ride can help maintain energy levels, though riders need to be careful not to overdo it, as slowing down to drink can cost valuable time.

Mastering time trials demands more than just strong legs. It is a complex blend of pacing, aerodynamics, equipment choice, mental fortitude, recovery strategy, and physical conditioning. Cyclists who wish to excel in time trials must fine-tune each of these elements through dedicated practice and experience, constantly refining their technique to shave off precious seconds.

Key Time Trial Races

Time trials feature prominently in many of the world's most prestigious cycling races, and they often serve as decisive stages where championships are won or lost.

These races test cyclists' ability to perform under pressure, relying on their skills to race against the clock. Among the most renowned time trials are those featured in the Tour de France, the Giro d'Italia, and the Vuelta a España.

The Tour de France, arguably the most famous cycling race in the world, includes several individual time trials (known as ITTs) each year. The significance of these time trials cannot be understated—they often determine the overall winner of the race. One notable example is the 1989 Tour de France, when Greg LeMond secured victory in the final time trial stage by just eight seconds, the smallest margin in the race's history. The drama and excitement surrounding time trials in the Tour de France make them unforgettable moments in cycling history. Cyclists who can dominate these stages often have a huge advantage in the overall classification.

The Giro d'Italia, another Grand Tour, is known for its challenging and technical time trial stages. While the Giro typically features long, grueling mountain stages, the time trials inject a different type of difficulty into the race. Riders need to balance their performance in the mountains with their ability to maintain speed and endurance in time trials. The combination of high-altitude climbs and fast-paced time trials tests a cyclist's versatility. Recent editions of the Giro have featured both flat time trials, where speed and aerodynamics are key, and hilly time trials, where pacing and climbing ability come into play.

The Vuelta a España, Spain's premier cycling race, also includes critical time trial stages. Like the Giro and Tour de France, the Vuelta's time trials are often decisive. In the 2019 edition of the Vuelta, Primož Roglič himself showcased his incredible time trial skills, gaining enough time in the stage to secure his overall victory. The Vuelta's time trials tend to be particularly challenging due to the Spanish heat and tough terrain, which adds an extra layer of difficulty to an already demanding discipline.

Outside of the Grand Tours, the UCI Road World Championships also hold a prestigious time trial event. The individual time trial in the World Championships is a standalone race, where the best cyclists from around the globe compete for the coveted rainbow jersey. Winning this event marks a cyclist as one of the best time trialists in the world, and the race has been won by legends of the sport, such as Tony Martin and Fabian Cancellara. Unlike the time trials in the Grand Tours, which are part of a multi-stage event, the World Championship time trial is a one-off race, requiring cyclists to be at their absolute best on that day.

These key races are not just about individual victories—they are where champions are made. Winning a time trial in a major event can boost a cyclist's career, giving them a reputation for being able to perform under pressure. For many cyclists, mastering these races is essential if they want to be considered among the elite.

Analyzing Rivals and Strategies

In competitive time trials, understanding the strengths and weaknesses of one's rivals can be just as important as personal preparation. Analyzing competitors provides insights into how they might approach the race, and it allows cyclists to adjust their own strategies accordingly. The art of time trials involves not just riding fast but also outsmarting the competition.

One of the key aspects of analyzing rivals is studying their past performances. Cyclists and their teams will carefully review how a competitor has performed in previous time trials to identify patterns in their pacing or tendencies. For example, some cyclists are known for starting fast and slowing down toward the end of the race, while others might conserve energy early and finish with a burst of speed. By recognizing these tendencies, a cyclist can adjust their own pacing strategy to exploit their rival's weaknesses.

The equipment used by rivals can also provide valuable clues. A change in a competitor's bike setup, such as switching to more aerodynamic components or adjusting their riding position, could indicate a new focus on time trials. These changes can signal that the rival is aiming to improve their performance in specific conditions, whether it's a flat, fast course or a hilly, technical one. Keeping an eye on such details can give cyclists an edge, helping them anticipate how their opponents will tackle the course.

Psychological factors play a big role in time trial races. While the clock is the primary opponent, the mental game between competitors is always present. Some cyclists perform better under pressure, while others struggle when they're expected to deliver a top result. Understanding a rival's mental state before a race can help a cyclist form their strategy. If a competitor is known for cracking under pressure, the goal might be to put in an early, strong effort to create a psychological challenge. On the other hand, if a competitor is known for their mental toughness, a more calculated, controlled approach might be the best strategy.

CHAPTER 5: GRAND TOURS AND MAJOR VICTORIES

Breakthrough at the Vuelta a España

For Primož Roglič, the Vuelta a España was the stage where he truly began to establish himself as one of the top cyclists in the world. The Vuelta, one of cycling's three Grand Tours, provided Roglič with the perfect platform to showcase his abilities across a range of grueling terrains, and it was where he cemented his status as a rider capable of taking on the best in the sport.

Roglič's breakthrough at the Vuelta a España didn't come overnight. It was the result of years of hard work, perseverance, and determination to succeed in the highly competitive world of professional cycling. Before arriving at the Vuelta, Roglič had already shown promise in other races, but it was this Spanish tour that would prove to be the pivotal moment in his career. The race itself, spanning three weeks and covering mountains, flat roads, and time trials, is regarded as one of the toughest on the cycling calendar. It's a true test of a rider's endurance, strength, and mental toughness.

In 2019, Roglič arrived at the Vuelta with a growing reputation as a strong rider, particularly in time trials. Yet, few could have predicted the extent of his success that year. The first week of the race saw Roglič establishing himself among the front-runners, performing well in the individual stages and staying in close contention with the other favorites. His calm demeanor and steady approach to racing kept him consistent, and it became clear early on that he was not going to fade as the race progressed.

The turning point in the Vuelta came during the individual time trial stage. Roglič, known for his skill in this discipline, delivered a stunning performance, gaining significant time over his rivals. This stage victory put him in the leader's red jersey, a position he would hold for much of the remainder of the race. Time trials are often considered Roglič's strength, and he used this ability to his advantage, building a commanding lead that would prove crucial in the later stages.

But the Vuelta is not just about time trials; it also demands excellence in climbing. Roglič showed that he was more than capable of handling the high-altitude mountain stages. These stages are often where the race is won or lost, as the extreme inclines test the physical limits of even the best cyclists. Roglič's ability to maintain his pace on the steepest climbs, coupled with his strategic race management, allowed him to fend off challenges from other top riders. Each mountain stage became a tactical battle, with Roglič using his knowledge of the terrain and his team's support to maintain his lead.

As the race neared its conclusion, Roglič faced several challenges from competitors hoping to knock him off the top spot. The Vuelta's unpredictability, with its harsh weather conditions and unpredictable course routes, made it a difficult race to control. However, Roglič remained composed, relying on his physical fitness and mental toughness to see him through. His focus and determination allowed him to handle the pressure of leading one of the world's biggest races.

By the time the Vuelta reached its final stage in Madrid, Roglič had done enough to secure his first Grand Tour victory. It was a historic moment for him and for Slovenia, as he became the first Slovenian cyclist to win a Grand Tour. The victory at the Vuelta not only demonstrated Roglič's talent but also marked his arrival as a major contender in the sport of cycling.

This breakthrough win was an attestation to Roglič's journey from a former ski jumper to one of the most versatile cyclists in the world. His victory at the Vuelta established him as a rider to watch in future races and laid the foundation for his subsequent successes in other Grand Tours. It also showcased his ability to adapt and grow as a cyclist, as he learned from past races and refined his approach to achieve this major victory.

The Challenge of the Tour de France

Following his breakthrough at the Vuelta a España, Primož Roglič turned his focus to the Tour de France, the most prestigious race in the cycling world. Winning the Tour is considered the ultimate achievement for any cyclist, but it is also one of the most difficult feats to accomplish. The Tour de France, with its three weeks of intense racing, is a grueling test of endurance, skill, and strategy. For Roglič, the challenge of the Tour would push him to his limits and test every aspect of his ability as a rider.

Roglič entered the Tour de France with high expectations. Having proven his ability to win a Grand Tour at the Vuelta, many believed that he had the potential to compete for the yellow jersey, awarded to the overall winner of the Tour. However, the Tour de France is a completely different beast from other races. The course is known for its difficult mountain stages, unpredictable weather conditions, and the sheer number of competitors, all of whom are aiming for the top prize. Even with his success at the Vuelta, Roglič knew that winning the Tour would require an even greater effort.

One of the main challenges of the Tour de France is its demanding course. The race typically includes multiple stages in the Alps and the Pyrenees, where the steep climbs test a cyclist's ability to handle long, grueling ascents. Roglič, who had shown his strength in the mountains during the Vuelta, prepared meticulously for these stages. He worked on his climbing technique, ensuring that he could maintain a steady pace even on the steepest slopes. But climbing is only one part of the challenge. The Tour de France also requires riders to navigate long, flat stages and time trials, where aerodynamics and pacing are critical.

Another challenge Roglič faced was the competition. The Tour de France attracts the best cyclists from around the world, and every rider comes to the race with the goal of winning. The presence of multiple contenders makes it difficult for any one rider to dominate the race. Roglič had to contend with rivals who were just as determined and talented, and the tactics used by his competitors often influenced the outcome of each stage. In the Tour, cyclists must constantly be aware of their rivals' positions and adjust their strategies accordingly. A single mistake in judgment or a moment of hesitation can cost a rider valuable time.

The mental challenge of the Tour de France cannot be underestimated. For three weeks, riders must stay focused on the race, dealing with the physical exhaustion that builds up over time. Each stage presents new obstacles, and the pressure to perform at a high level every day can take a toll on even the most experienced riders. For Roglič, maintaining his mental sharpness throughout the race was crucial. He knew that one bad day could ruin his chances of winning the overall classification, so he approached each stage with a clear plan and a determined mindset.

Despite the challenges, Roglič's performances in the Tour de France have been impressive. In 2020, he came agonizingly close to winning the race, only to lose the yellow jersey in the final time trial to fellow Slovenian Tadej Pogačar. It was a heartbreaking moment for Roglič, as he had led the race for much of the final week and seemed poised to claim victory. The defeat was a reminder of just how difficult it is to win the Tour de France, where even the smallest mistake can have huge consequences.

Celebrating Milestones in Major Tours

Over the course of his career, Primož Roglič has achieved numerous milestones in major cycling tours, solidifying his status as one of the top riders in the world. From his breakthrough at the Vuelta a España to his near-victory at the Tour de France, Roglič's journey in the world of professional cycling has been filled with unforgettable moments.

One of the most significant milestones in Roglič's career was his first Grand Tour victory at the 2019 Vuelta a España. This win was a turning point, marking the beginning of Roglič's dominance in Grand Tours. Winning the Vuelta not only demonstrated his ability to compete at the highest level but also gave him the confidence to take on even greater challenges in the future. The Vuelta win was celebrated not just in the cycling world but also in Slovenia, where Roglič became a national hero.

Another key milestone came with Roglič's success in the 2021 Vuelta a España, where he defended his title for the third consecutive year. This achievement was particularly noteworthy because it placed him in an elite group of riders who have won the same Grand Tour multiple times. Winning the Vuelta three times in a row is a rare feat, and it highlighted Roglič's consistency and ability to perform under pressure. Each victory was hard-fought, with different challenges in each edition of the race, but Roglič's ability to adapt and overcome these challenges set him apart from his competitors.

Roglič's performances in the Tour de France also represent important milestones in his career. Although he has yet to win the Tour, his second-place finish in 2020 remains one of the highlights of his career. The Tour is widely regarded as the toughest race in the world, and Roglič's ability to compete at the highest level against the best riders in the world has earned him respect and admiration from fans and fellow cyclists alike. His near-victory in 2020 was a bittersweet moment, but it also served as a reminder of his incredible talent and determination.

In addition to his Grand Tour victories, Roglič has celebrated milestones in other major races, such as his victories in prestigious one-week tours like the Critérium du Dauphiné and Tirreno-Adriatico. These races, while shorter than the Grand Tours, are important tests of a rider's all-around abilities, and Roglič's success in these events has further solidified his reputation as one of the most versatile cyclists in the world.

CHAPTER 6: OVERCOMING ADVERSITY

Injuries and Setbacks

Every athlete, no matter how talented or determined, faces challenges throughout their career. For Primož Roglič, injuries and setbacks have been a significant part of his journey. While his success as a professional cyclist is undeniable, his path to the top has not been without its struggles. In fact, these moments of adversity have helped shape him into the resilient and focused competitor he is today.

One of the most difficult aspects of being a professional cyclist is the physical toll that the sport takes on the body. Cycling, especially at the level of Grand Tours, demands incredible endurance and strength. Riders push their bodies to the limit for hours each day, often across difficult terrains. Over time, this level of physical exertion can lead to injuries. Roglič has not been immune to this reality. Throughout his career, he has faced a number of injuries that have threatened to derail his progress.

One of the most significant setbacks for Roglič occurred in 2021 during the Tour de France. Early in the race, he suffered a crash that resulted in several injuries, including bruises and cuts. Although Roglič initially tried to continue, the pain and the physical damage from the crash eventually forced him to withdraw from the race. It was a heartbreaking moment for Roglič, who had entered the Tour as one of the favorites to win. His withdrawal marked the end of his hopes for that year's Tour, and it was a bitter reminder of how quickly fortunes can change in professional cycling.

The nature of cycling means that crashes are not uncommon. Riders often travel at high speeds, sometimes in tight groups, and the risk of accidents is always present. For Roglič, the 2021 Tour de France crash was a particularly painful setback, not just physically but emotionally. Having prepared extensively for the race, the crash and subsequent withdrawal were devastating. Yet, like many athletes, Roglič has learned to deal with such setbacks and use them as motivation to come back stronger.

Injuries, however, are not always the result of crashes. The repetitive nature of cycling can lead to overuse injuries, where certain parts of the body, such as the knees or back, experience strain from the constant motion. Over the years, Roglič has had to manage various physical issues that arise from the sheer volume of training and racing. Professional cyclists spend countless hours on the bike, and this can lead to wear and tear on the body. For Roglič, staying on top of his physical condition has been a key part of his ability to remain competitive at the highest level.

Managing injuries is not just about dealing with the pain in the moment. It also involves a long process of recovery and rehabilitation. When athletes suffer injuries, they are often forced to take time away from their sport to allow their bodies to heal. This can be frustrating, especially for someone as driven as Roglič, who is used to training hard and competing regularly. The recovery process requires patience and discipline, as rushing back too soon can lead to further complications.

Roglič's experience with injuries has taught him the importance of taking the necessary time to recover fully. While it can be tempting to return to racing as quickly as possible, especially with major competitions like the Tour de France or Vuelta a España on the horizon, Roglič understands that pushing too hard before his body is ready can result in even more significant setbacks. This is a lesson that many professional athletes learn over time – the body needs time to heal, and sometimes the best way to ensure future success is to take a step back and allow for proper recovery.

Despite the setbacks caused by injuries, Roglič has consistently shown an ability to bounce back. His determination to return to the top of his sport after each injury speaks to his resilience. Rather than allowing these setbacks to define his career, Roglič has used them as opportunities to learn and grow. Each time he has faced an injury, he has come back stronger, more focused, and more determined to succeed.

Injuries are an unavoidable part of professional sports, but they do not have to be the end of an athlete's story. For Roglič, the injuries he has endured have been challenging, but they have also been a key part of his development as a cyclist. Overcoming these physical setbacks has strengthened his resolve and given him a deeper appreciation for the moments when he is at full strength and able to compete at the highest level.

The road to recovery is never easy, but for Roglič, it has been a journey worth taking. His ability to overcome injuries and setbacks has been one of the defining aspects of his career, and it has earned him the respect and admiration of fans and fellow cyclists alike. In the world of professional cycling, where the margin between success and failure is often razor-thin, Roglič's perseverance in the face of adversity has set him apart as one of the sport's true champions.

Mental Toughness in Competition

In the world of professional sports, physical ability is only part of the equation. To succeed at the highest level, athletes must also possess incredible mental toughness. For Primož Roglič, mental strength has been just as important as his physical capabilities in overcoming challenges and achieving success. Throughout his career, Roglič has faced intense pressure, whether in the heat of competition or in the aftermath of setbacks like injuries. His ability to stay mentally strong, focus on his goals, and push through adversity has been a key factor in his rise to the top of the cycling world.

Cycling, especially at the level of Grand Tours, is as much a mental game as it is a physical one. Races like the Tour de France and the Vuelta a España are not won in a single day but over the course of several weeks. Each stage presents its own challenges, whether it's a steep mountain climb, a fast-paced flat stage, or a nerve-wracking time trial. Riders need to stay focused for hours at a time, all while managing their physical energy and making strategic decisions. For Roglič, the mental demands of cycling have required him to develop a level of toughness that allows him to stay calm under pressure and maintain his focus throughout each race.

One of the key aspects of mental toughness in cycling is the ability to handle setbacks and keep moving forward. In any race, there are moments when things don't go according to plan. Whether it's a crash, a mechanical problem, or simply a bad day on the bike, riders must learn to deal with these challenges without letting them derail their overall performance. For Roglič, the ability to stay mentally tough in the face of adversity has been one of the defining traits of his career.

For example, during the 2020 Tour de France, Roglič experienced one of the most heart-wrenching moments of his career. After leading the race for much of the final week, he lost the yellow jersey in the very last time trial to fellow Slovenian Tadej Pogačar. It was a crushing defeat, especially considering how close Roglič had come to winning the Tour. Many riders in his position might have struggled to recover mentally from such a setback, but Roglič showed remarkable resilience. Instead of dwelling on the loss, he used it as motivation to continue improving and pushing himself in future races.

Mental toughness also plays a crucial role in how athletes prepare for competition. For Roglič, maintaining focus during training and in the lead-up to major races is essential. The pressure to perform at the highest level can be immense, especially when the expectations are high, as they often are for a rider of Roglič's caliber. Yet, he has consistently demonstrated an ability to stay grounded and concentrate on the task at hand. Whether it's staying disciplined in his training routine or remaining calm in the days before a big race, Roglič's mental preparation has been key to his success.

Another aspect of mental toughness in cycling is the ability to endure pain and discomfort. Grand Tours are incredibly demanding, and riders often push their bodies to the limit in pursuit of victory. The ability to keep going, even when every muscle is screaming for rest, is a hallmark of a mentally tough athlete. Roglič's ability to dig deep during the most challenging moments of a race has been one of the reasons he has been able to compete at the highest level for so long.

Staying mentally tough in the face of competition also means knowing how to handle pressure. In the final stages of a race, when the stakes are at their highest, the pressure can be overwhelming. Yet, Roglič has repeatedly shown an ability to remain calm and composed, even in the most high-pressure situations. His ability to make smart decisions and stay focused on his goal, even when the competition is fierce, has been a key part of his success.

Mental toughness is about more than just handling pressure or overcoming setbacks. It's about having the inner strength to keep going, no matter what obstacles stand in the way. For Roglič, this has meant pushing through injuries, bouncing back from disappointing defeats, and continuing to strive for greatness, even when the odds are against him. His mental resilience has been one of the most important factors in his success, allowing him to overcome the challenges that inevitably come with a career in professional sports.

In the world of cycling, where races are often won or lost by mere seconds, mental toughness can make all the difference. For Roglič, his ability to stay strong mentally, both in and out of competition, has been a key part of his journey to the top of the sport. It has allowed him to overcome adversity, stay focused on his goals, and achieve success at the highest level of professional cycling.

Lessons Learned from Challenges

Throughout his career, Primož Roglič has faced numerous challenges, from injuries and crashes to heartbreaking defeats.

However, it is through these challenges that he has learned some of the most valuable lessons that have shaped him not only as a cyclist but as a person. Each setback has provided an opportunity for growth, teaching him how to overcome adversity and emerge stronger on the other side.

One of the most important lessons Roglič has learned is the value of perseverance. In a sport as demanding as cycling, there are always going to be moments when things don't go according to plan. Whether it's an injury that forces time away from competition or a loss that feels particularly crushing, Roglič has come to understand that success isn't always about winning every race. Instead, it's about the ability to keep going, even when the road gets tough.

His career is a testament to this mindset, as he has repeatedly bounced back from setbacks to achieve success.

For Roglič, perseverance isn't just about physical endurance; it's also about mental resilience. He has learned that staying focused on long-term goals is essential, even when short-term setbacks occur. This lesson was particularly evident in the aftermath of his 2020 Tour de France defeat. Rather than letting the loss define his career, Roglič used it as motivation to come back stronger. The following year, he won the Vuelta a España for the third time, proving that setbacks can serve as powerful catalysts for future success.

Another valuable lesson Roglič has learned is the importance of patience. In a sport where races can last for weeks, and seasons stretch across many months, it's easy to get caught up in the desire for immediate results. However, Roglič has come to understand that success often requires time and persistence. Whether it's recovering from an injury or building up the endurance needed for a Grand Tour, Roglič has learned that patience is key. This mindset has helped him navigate the inevitable ups and downs of his career, allowing him to stay focused on his goals even when progress seems slow.

Perhaps one of the most significant lessons Roglič has learned is the value of adaptability. In professional sports, things don't always go as planned, and athletes must be able to adjust to changing circumstances. For Roglič, this has meant learning how to adapt to physical setbacks, such as injuries, as well as mental challenges, such as dealing with the pressure of competition. His ability to stay flexible and adjust his approach when necessary has been a key factor in his success.

Roglič's journey has also taught him the importance of teamwork and support. While cycling is often seen as an individual sport, success at the highest level requires a strong team behind the rider. Roglič has learned that having a supportive team, both on and off the bike, is crucial to overcoming challenges. Whether it's the physical support of his teammates during a race or the emotional support of his family and friends during tough times, Roglič understands that he doesn't have to face challenges alone.

Through all the challenges he has faced, Roglič has also gained a deeper appreciation for the sport of cycling itself. The setbacks, the victories, the highs, and the lows have all contributed to his love for the sport. Rather than becoming discouraged by the difficulties he has encountered, Roglič has learned to embrace the journey. Each challenge has made his successes even more meaningful, as they have been hard-earned through perseverance, patience, and adaptability.

CHAPTER 7: THE ROLE OF TECHNOLOGY IN TRAINING

Advancements in Cycling Gear

In the world of professional cycling, one of the most noticeable changes over the years has been the significant advancements in cycling gear. From the bikes themselves to the clothing and accessories cyclists use, technology has transformed the sport, making it more efficient, safer, and more competitive. These advancements have become an essential part of modern training, helping athletes improve their performance and stay ahead of their competition.

One of the most important developments in cycling gear has been the evolution of the bicycle itself. In the early days of cycling, bikes were much heavier and less aerodynamic, making them harder to handle and slower on the road. Over the years, however, the materials used to make bikes have dramatically improved. Today, bikes are often made from lightweight carbon fiber, which is not only strong but also incredibly light. This allows cyclists to ride faster and more efficiently, especially during long races or uphill climbs. A lighter bike means less energy is spent just pushing it forward, which can make a big difference in performance over the course of a race.

Another key advancement in cycling gear is the design of helmets. Early helmets were mostly designed to protect the head in case of a fall, but they weren't particularly comfortable or aerodynamic. Modern helmets, however, are designed with both safety and performance in mind. They are built to be more aerodynamic, meaning they create less wind resistance as the cyclist moves forward. This small change can add up over the course of a long ride, helping cyclists maintain higher speeds. Additionally, today's helmets are more comfortable and better ventilated, which can be crucial for keeping a rider cool during a long race in the heat.

Cycling shoes have also seen major improvements. In the past, cyclists often wore regular shoes while riding, which didn't offer much support or control. Today, specialized cycling shoes are designed to clip directly into the pedals of the bike, giving the rider more power and control with each pedal stroke. These shoes are often made from lightweight materials, making them comfortable to wear for long periods. The stiff soles help ensure that as much energy as possible is transferred from the rider's legs to the bike, which can lead to more efficient riding.

Even the clothing that cyclists wear has undergone significant changes. Modern cycling jerseys and shorts are made from materials that are both lightweight and breathable, helping to regulate the rider's body temperature. These clothes are also designed to reduce wind resistance, making it easier for cyclists to move quickly through the air. Some jerseys are even embedded with special fabrics that can help wick sweat away from the body, keeping riders dry and comfortable during long rides.

A relatively recent innovation in cycling gear is the use of electronic shifting. In the past, cyclists had to manually shift gears by moving levers on their bike. This could be difficult and time-consuming, especially during a fast race. Today, many high-end bikes come with electronic shifting systems that allow riders to change gears with just the press of a button. This makes it easier to quickly adjust to different terrains, such as going from a flat road to a steep hill, without losing momentum.

Another technological advancement in cycling gear is the use of power meters. These devices, which are often built into the bike's pedals or crank, measure how much power a cyclist is generating with each pedal stroke. This information is incredibly valuable for training, as it allows cyclists to track their performance in real time. By knowing how much power they are producing, riders can adjust their effort during a race to avoid burning out too early or pushing too hard when it's not necessary.

In addition to power meters, cyclists today also rely on advanced GPS devices to help with training. These devices, which are usually mounted on the handlebars of the bike, can track the rider's speed, distance, and elevation, as well as provide real-time directions. This is especially useful for long training rides in unfamiliar areas. GPS devices also allow cyclists to analyze their performance after a ride, giving them valuable data that can be used to improve future rides.

Perhaps one of the most overlooked advancements in cycling gear is the improvement in bike tires. In the past, tires were often made from rubber that wasn't particularly durable, leading to frequent flats or other issues. Today's tires are made from more advanced materials that are not only more durable but also provide better traction and control. Some tires are even designed to be resistant to punctures, which can be a lifesaver during a long race. The width of tires has also changed, with many cyclists now opting for wider tires that offer more stability and grip, especially on rough or wet roads.

All of these advancements in cycling gear have had a profound impact on the sport. They have made it easier for cyclists to train more effectively, push their limits, and achieve higher levels of performance. As technology continues to evolve, it's likely that we'll see even more innovations in the years to come, further shaping the future of cycling.

Data Analysis and Performance Metrics

In modern cycling, data has become a key component of training and performance. Gone are the days when cyclists would simply rely on how they felt during a ride to gauge their performance. Today, advanced tools allow riders and their coaches to gather detailed data about every aspect of their training, providing valuable insights that can help them improve and fine-tune their performance.

One of the most important types of data used in cycling is power output. Power is measured in watts and reflects how much energy a cyclist is putting into each pedal stroke. By using power meters, cyclists can track their power output in real time during a ride. This data is crucial for training, as it allows riders to understand how hard they are working at any given moment. For example, if a cyclist knows they can sustain 250 watts for a certain period of time, they can use that information to pace themselves during a race. This prevents them from going too hard too soon or not pushing themselves hard enough when it matters most.

In addition to power, cyclists also track their heart rate during training. Heart rate monitors, which are often worn as chest straps or wristbands, provide real-time data on how fast the rider's heart is beating. This information is useful because it gives an indication of how hard the rider's body is working. By comparing heart rate data with power output, cyclists can see how efficiently their bodies are performing. For example, if a cyclist's heart rate is lower than usual for a given power output, it might mean they are becoming more efficient and stronger. Conversely, a higher-than-normal heart rate for the same power output could indicate fatigue or the need for more recovery.

Another important metric in cycling is cadence, which refers to how fast a cyclist is pedaling. Cadence is measured in revolutions per minute (RPM) and is a key factor in determining how efficiently a rider is using their energy. Cyclists can use cadence data to find their optimal pedaling speed. For example, some riders perform best with a high cadence, while others prefer a slower, more powerful pedal stroke. By analyzing cadence data, cyclists can make adjustments to their technique to improve their efficiency and performance.

Cyclists also use speed and distance data to track their progress over time. GPS devices, which are mounted on the handlebars, provide real-time data on how fast the rider is going and how far they've traveled. This information is particularly useful for tracking improvements in performance. For example, if a rider consistently completes a certain training route at a faster speed, it's a good indication that their fitness level is improving.

Elevation data is another important metric, especially for cyclists who train in hilly or mountainous areas. GPS devices can track how much elevation a rider gains during a ride, which provides valuable insights into how well they handle climbs. Cyclists can use this data to compare their performance on different types of terrain and adjust their training accordingly. For example, if a rider struggles on steep climbs, they can focus on improving their climbing ability by incorporating more hill training into their routine.

Data analysis doesn't stop once the ride is over. Many cyclists use software programs to analyze their performance in detail. These programs allow riders to upload data from their power meters, heart rate monitors, and GPS devices, providing a comprehensive overview of their training. Cyclists can review metrics such as power, speed, and heart rate over the course of a ride, identifying areas where they can improve. For example, if a rider notices that their power output drops significantly during the final part of a ride, they might need to work on their endurance.

Coaches also play a key role in data analysis. By reviewing a rider's data, coaches can provide targeted feedback and develop training plans that address specific areas of weakness. For example, if a rider's cadence is too low during climbs, a coach might suggest drills to improve their pedal stroke. Or if a rider's heart rate is too high during long efforts, the coach might adjust their training to focus on building endurance.

In addition to improving individual performance, data analysis also plays a role in team strategy. In professional cycling, teams often use data to make tactical decisions during races. For example, by analyzing power and speed data, teams can determine when it's the best time for a rider to attack or conserve energy. This data-driven approach to strategy has become increasingly important in the highly competitive world of professional cycling.

Innovations Shaping Modern Cycling

The sport of cycling has always been influenced by technology, but in recent years, innovations have taken the sport to a whole new level. These advancements aren't just limited to the bikes themselves but extend to training techniques, nutrition, and race strategies. As a result, modern cyclists are able to achieve performance levels that were unimaginable just a few decades ago.

One of the most significant innovations in modern cycling is the use of wind tunnel testing. In the past, cyclists would rely on trial and error to find the most aerodynamic position on their bikes. Today, however, wind tunnel testing allows riders to fine-tune their position with scientific precision. By riding in a wind tunnel, cyclists can see how different body positions and gear choices affect their aerodynamic profile. This information helps them minimize drag, which can make a significant difference in performance, especially in time trials or long races where maintaining high speeds is critical.

Another major innovation in cycling is the use of smart trainers for indoor training. Smart trainers are devices that attach to a bike's rear wheel and provide resistance, simulating outdoor riding conditions. These trainers are connected to software programs that allow riders to follow virtual routes or participate in structured workouts. The benefit of smart trainers is that they allow cyclists to train indoors while still experiencing the same physical demands as outdoor riding. This is particularly useful during bad weather or when it's not possible to train outside. Smart trainers also provide real-time data on power, speed, and cadence, allowing cyclists to track their progress during each workout.

Virtual racing has also become increasingly popular in recent years. Using platforms like Zwift, cyclists can compete against other riders from around the world in real-time virtual races. These races are held on virtual courses that simulate real-world conditions, such as hills and wind resistance. Virtual racing allows cyclists to test their skills and endurance in a competitive environment, even if they can't participate in outdoor races. It also provides a new way for cyclists to stay motivated and engaged during training, as they can race against friends or strangers from the comfort of their own homes.

Nutrition has also seen significant advancements in modern cycling. In the past, cyclists would rely on simple foods like bananas or sandwiches during long rides. Today, however, sports nutrition has become much more advanced. Cyclists now use specially formulated energy gels, drinks, and bars that are designed to provide the optimal balance of carbohydrates, proteins, and electrolytes. These products are designed to be easily digestible and provide a quick source of energy, helping riders maintain their performance during long races or intense training sessions.

Recovery techniques have also evolved with the help of technology. Cyclists now use tools like foam rollers, massage guns, and compression garments to aid in recovery after a hard workout or race. These tools help reduce muscle soreness and promote faster recovery, allowing riders to get back to training more quickly. In addition, many cyclists use recovery apps that provide guided stretching and mobility routines, helping them stay flexible and prevent injuries.

One of the most exciting innovations in cycling is the use of artificial intelligence (AI) in training. AI-powered coaching platforms analyze a rider's data and provide personalized training plans based on their goals and performance. These platforms can adjust workouts in real-time, providing immediate feedback and recommendations. For example, if a cyclist is struggling with a particular aspect of their training, the AI coach might suggest a different type of workout or a new approach to their training. This personalized approach helps cyclists stay on track and make continuous improvements.

As technology continues to evolve, the future of cycling looks incredibly promising. Innovations in gear, training techniques, and performance analysis are likely to continue shaping the sport in new and exciting ways. For cyclists at all levels, these advancements offer new opportunities to train smarter, ride faster, and achieve their personal best. Whether it's through aerodynamic improvements, advanced data analysis, or cutting-edge recovery techniques, the role of technology in cycling has never been more important.

CHAPTER 8: LIFE BEYOND THE BIKE

Personal Life and Interests

For any athlete, the sport they dedicate their lives to can become all-consuming. The long hours of training, traveling to competitions, and constantly working to maintain peak performance leave little room for much else. But even for top athletes, life outside the sport is important. For cyclists, who spend countless hours on the road or in the mountains, finding balance in their personal life is essential for their mental and emotional well-being. In this chapter, we'll take a closer look at the personal side of a professional cyclist's life, exploring their interests beyond cycling and how they unwind after intense races.

For most cyclists, family is a key part of their lives off the bike. Whether it's spending time with a partner, raising children, or visiting extended family, many athletes prioritize their relationships when they aren't racing. After all, cycling careers, like most in professional sports, can be physically and mentally demanding. Spending time with loved ones offers a way to relax and recharge. It helps them stay grounded, especially when the pressures of competition begin to weigh heavily. Many cyclists talk about how important it is to return home to the comfort of family after a grueling race season.

Cyclists also often have interests and hobbies outside of their sport, providing a much-needed mental break from the physical and tactical demands of racing. Some cyclists are drawn to outdoor activities, which isn't surprising given their love for nature. Hiking, skiing, and even fishing are popular pastimes that allow them to explore nature without the competitive intensity of racing. For those who live near mountains or lakes, these activities offer a chance to reconnect with the outdoors in a more relaxed setting.

Beyond outdoor activities, many cyclists have artistic or creative interests. Some enjoy photography, taking time to capture the beautiful landscapes they travel through during their races. Others might have a passion for music, playing an instrument or even learning a new one during their downtime. Having these hobbies provides a creative outlet that can relieve stress and offer a sense of accomplishment outside of cycling. It also gives them something to look forward to once their racing careers eventually come to an end.

Travel is another common interest among cyclists. While much of their travel is centered around competitions, many take the opportunity to explore new places during their time off. Racing in different countries and cities exposes cyclists to a variety of cultures, foods, and traditions. When their racing schedules allow it, they often enjoy immersing themselves in the local culture, whether it's by trying regional dishes or learning about the history of the area. For many cyclists, these experiences leave a lasting impact, broadening their perspective on the world and enriching their personal lives.

Fitness remains an important part of many cyclists' lives outside of racing, but they often enjoy trying different forms of exercise that aren't related to cycling. Some take up yoga or pilates to improve their flexibility and strength, while others might explore running or swimming as a way to stay active without the wear and tear of cycling. These activities help maintain their physical health while providing a refreshing change from their usual training routines.

Friendships formed outside of cycling also play a significant role in their personal lives. Many cyclists have friends who aren't involved in the sport, which can be refreshing as it offers them a chance to engage in conversations that aren't centered around cycling. Spending time with friends who have different interests and perspectives provides a break from the single-minded focus that competitive cycling requires.

Many cyclists are deeply connected to their communities. Whether it's by attending local events, volunteering, or simply being involved in neighborhood activities, they find ways to contribute to the places they call home. Being part of a community helps cyclists maintain a sense of normalcy and connection, especially after returning from long periods of travel.

While cycling is a major part of their lives, these athletes also recognize the importance of maintaining a well-rounded personal life. It helps them manage the pressures of competition and brings them happiness in areas outside of sport. By spending time with family, pursuing creative hobbies, traveling, staying fit, and connecting with their communities, cyclists find joy in the many facets of life beyond the bike.

Philanthropy and Giving Back

Cycling is a sport that provides not only a sense of personal accomplishment but also a platform to make a positive difference in the world. Many cyclists, as they become more successful, feel a strong desire to give back to their communities and contribute to causes that are close to their hearts. Philanthropy often becomes a significant part of their lives beyond racing, with some cyclists even founding charitable organizations to support various initiatives.

One of the most common ways cyclists give back is through fundraising. Many riders participate in charity rides, where the goal is not only to race but to raise money for a specific cause. These events bring together both professional and amateur cyclists, with participants riding for something bigger than just winning. The causes they support can vary widely, from funding medical research to supporting local youth programs. For many cyclists, the opportunity to use their platform to raise awareness and funds for important causes is deeply fulfilling.

Some cyclists have personal reasons for choosing the causes they support. For example, they may have a family member who has battled a serious illness, or they may have witnessed social injustices firsthand. These experiences often inspire them to use their fame and resources to advocate for change and make a difference in areas that matter most to them. Whether it's supporting cancer research, mental health awareness, or environmental sustainability, cyclists are in a unique position to bring attention to important social issues.

In addition to participating in charity rides and fundraisers, some cyclists go a step further by creating their own foundations. These organizations often focus on issues that the cyclists are particularly passionate about, whether it's promoting health and fitness, helping underprivileged children, or protecting the environment. Through their foundations, cyclists can have a direct impact on the causes they care about, often partnering with other organizations to maximize their reach and effectiveness.

One of the key reasons why many cyclists engage in philanthropy is because they understand the influence they have as public figures. Their successes on the bike allow them to reach a broad audience, and they often feel a sense of responsibility to use their platform for good. By supporting causes that align with their values, cyclists can inspire their fans and followers to take action as well. This ripple effect allows them to amplify their impact and contribute to meaningful change in the world.

Cyclists are also involved in community outreach programs, particularly those focused on promoting cycling as a healthy and sustainable mode of transportation. They often partner with schools, local governments, and non-profit organizations to encourage cycling as a way to combat pollution, reduce traffic congestion, and improve public health. These initiatives aim to make cycling more accessible to people of all ages and abilities, particularly in urban areas where traffic and pollution are major concerns.

In addition to their charitable efforts, many cyclists serve as role models for the next generation of athletes. They take time to mentor young cyclists, offering advice and guidance on everything from training and nutrition to handling the pressures of competition. For many young athletes, having a professional cyclist as a mentor can be incredibly motivating and inspiring. It shows them that with hard work and dedication, they too can achieve their dreams.

Giving back isn't just about financial contributions or public events; many cyclists also dedicate time to volunteer work. Whether it's visiting hospitals, speaking at schools, or participating in local clean-up efforts, they find ways to give their time and energy to help others. These acts of kindness, though sometimes less visible than large charity events, are just as impactful and demonstrate the deep sense of responsibility that many cyclists feel toward their communities.

Future Aspirations Beyond Cycling

For many professional cyclists, the idea of what comes next after their cycling career is something they think about early on. Unlike many other professions, cycling has a relatively short career span, with most riders retiring from competitive racing by their late 30s or early 40s. This means that cyclists often need to plan for their future well in advance. While some might choose to stay within the cycling world, others look to pursue entirely new paths that allow them to explore different passions and interests.

One of the most common paths for retired cyclists is to transition into coaching or team management. With years of experience and knowledge gained from competing at the highest level, many cyclists are well-equipped to guide the next generation of riders. Coaching allows them to stay connected to the sport they love while also sharing their expertise with younger athletes. Some cyclists become team directors, helping to manage professional cycling teams and make strategic decisions during races. Others may choose to open cycling academies or training centers where they can work directly with aspiring cyclists, helping them develop their skills and navigate the competitive world of cycling.

Another path that many cyclists pursue is media work. As experts in the sport, former cyclists are often sought after as commentators or analysts for cycling events. Their insider knowledge of the sport allows them to provide unique insights into race strategies, tactics, and the mental and physical demands of cycling. Some cyclists even go on to write books about their experiences, sharing stories from their careers and offering advice to aspiring athletes. Others may work as broadcasters, hosting cycling-related shows or podcasts that explore the latest developments in the sport.

Beyond the world of cycling, many athletes develop new careers in business or entrepreneurship. Some cyclists start their own companies, often related to their passion for fitness or sports. Whether it's launching a line of cycling gear, opening a bike shop, or creating a fitness app, these ventures allow cyclists to channel their competitive spirit into new and exciting opportunities. Others may choose to invest in existing businesses, using their financial success from cycling to support start-ups or other ventures they believe in.

Education is another area where many cyclists choose to focus their future aspirations. Some return to school after their racing careers, pursuing degrees in fields like business, sports management, or even completely unrelated areas like law or medicine. For those who have spent most of their lives focused on sport, education offers a chance to develop new skills and explore new career opportunities. Whether they're interested in pursuing a second career in a different industry or simply expanding their knowledge, many cyclists find fulfillment in continuing their education after retirement.

For some cyclists, retirement offers the opportunity to focus on personal projects that they may not have had time for during their careers. Whether it's writing, art, or travel, these projects allow them to explore their creative side and pursue passions outside of cycling. Many athletes enjoy the freedom that comes with retirement, using it as a chance to finally relax and enjoy life at a slower pace after years of intense competition.

Many cyclists look forward to spending more time with their families after retirement. The demanding travel schedules and long hours of training required in professional cycling can make it difficult to fully engage in family life. Retirement offers a chance to reconnect with loved ones, whether it's by spending more time at home, traveling together, or simply enjoying the everyday moments that they may have missed during their racing careers.

CHAPTER 9: LEGACY AND IMPACT ON THE SPORT

Inspiring a New Generation of Cyclists

Primož Roglič's journey from ski jumping to becoming one of the most successful cyclists in the world has become a source of inspiration for countless young athletes. His story is not just about his impressive wins but also about the determination and resilience he demonstrated throughout his career. His rise to the top, especially considering that he came to cycling later than most professional riders, shows that it's never too late to chase your dreams. For many young people, Roglič has become a symbol of hard work, passion, and persistence.

Cycling, like any sport, demands years of training, physical endurance, and mental strength. But Roglič's path was anything but typical. Before becoming a cyclist, he was a ski jumper, competing at a high level in that sport. However, after a serious fall, he shifted his focus to cycling, a sport he had no professional background in. Despite this late start, Roglič rapidly improved and soon became one of the best in the world. His ability to transition from one sport to another and then excel at the highest levels has inspired young athletes to believe that they, too, can succeed in ways they might not have imagined.

For many young cyclists, Roglič's success is a reminder that the road to greatness is rarely straightforward. His setbacks, injuries, and challenges didn't deter him; instead, they motivated him to push harder. The younger generation of riders can look to Roglič as an example of how to handle adversity. Whether it was his late start in cycling or his unfortunate crashes during important races, he never gave up. His tenacity, even in the face of difficulties, serves as a valuable lesson: success isn't just about talent; it's about how you respond when things go wrong.

Roglič's influence extends beyond Slovenia, reaching young cyclists across the globe. His success in major races like the Tour de France, Vuelta a España, and Giro d'Italia has made him a household name in the cycling world. Aspiring cyclists from different countries now look up to him, hoping to follow in his footsteps. They see a rider who faced setbacks but kept moving forward, and that resonates deeply. In interviews, Roglič often emphasizes the importance of perseverance, encouraging young athletes to believe in themselves and keep working hard, even when the odds seem stacked against them.

Roglič has shown that you don't need to come from a traditional cycling background to make it to the top. Many professional cyclists start riding competitively at a young age, often joining cycling clubs in their teens or even earlier. Roglič, on the other hand, made his switch to cycling in his twenties. This unconventional path sends a powerful message to young athletes: your background doesn't determine your future. What matters most is the dedication you bring to the table once you decide to pursue something.

For the new generation of cyclists, Roglič is not just a champion but also a role model. His dedication to his craft, his sportsmanship, and his humility off the bike make him a figure to admire. He remains approachable, often taking time to meet with fans, sign autographs, and share words of encouragement. These interactions leave a lasting impression on young cyclists who may dream of becoming professional riders themselves. Roglič's down-to-earth nature makes him even more relatable, proving that even at the top, athletes can stay humble and connected to their fans.

One of the key ways Roglič has inspired young cyclists is through his performances in major races. His victories in the Vuelta a España, where he won multiple editions, have cemented his status as one of the sport's greats. These victories were not just important for his career; they became moments of celebration for his fans and aspiring cyclists worldwide. Each win showcased his resilience, tactical acumen, and physical endurance, qualities that young riders strive to emulate.

Another significant aspect of Roglič's influence is the way he approaches his training and preparation. Young cyclists often look for guidance on how to balance their lives with the demands of the sport. Roglič has spoken openly about his training routines, mental preparation, and the importance of rest and recovery. His disciplined approach to cycling is something that young riders can learn from, understanding that success in the sport requires more than just talent; it requires careful planning, mental toughness, and the ability to recover both physically and mentally.

Roglič's legacy will likely continue to inspire future generations of cyclists for years to come. His journey proves that with the right mindset, determination, and hard work, it's possible to overcome the odds and achieve great things, even in a demanding sport like cycling. Young riders around the world will continue to look to him as an example of what can be achieved when you put your heart and soul into your passion.

Contributions to Slovenian Cycling

Before Primož Roglič and his compatriot Tadej Pogačar became global cycling stars, Slovenia wasn't widely recognized as a major player in the world of professional cycling. While the country had produced talented athletes in other sports, cycling was not traditionally seen as a field where Slovenian athletes would dominate. That changed with the rise of Roglič, whose remarkable achievements have placed Slovenia firmly on the map in the world of cycling.

Roglič's success has brought unprecedented attention to Slovenian cycling, inspiring a wave of interest and participation in the sport within the country. As Roglič started winning major races, more and more young Slovenians began taking up cycling, seeing it as a viable path to international success. Local cycling clubs have reported increased enrollment, with many young riders dreaming of following in Roglič's footsteps. His achievements have created a cultural shift, where cycling has become a popular and respected sport in Slovenia, much like football or basketball in other countries.

One of Roglič's most significant contributions to Slovenian cycling has been his role as a trailblazer. Before his rise, there was little expectation that Slovenian cyclists could compete at the same level as riders from more established cycling nations like France, Spain, or Italy. Roglič shattered that perception, proving that with hard work, determination, and the right support, Slovenian athletes could excel in the sport. His success has paved the way for future generations of Slovenian cyclists, who now see the possibility of competing on the world stage.

Roglič's influence has also extended to the infrastructure of Slovenian cycling. His success has sparked a renewed interest in developing cycling facilities, creating more opportunities for young riders to train and compete. Local governments and private sponsors have become more interested in supporting cycling events, funding programs that provide training for young athletes, and building new cycling tracks. Roglič's achievements have helped drive these changes, showing that investment in cycling can yield tremendous results.

Additionally, Roglič has played a role in raising the profile of Slovenian cycling through his international presence. When he competes in races like the Tour de France or the Vuelta a España, he carries the Slovenian flag with him, bringing attention to his home country. His victories are celebrated not just by cycling fans but by Slovenians across the nation, who take pride in his accomplishments. These moments of national pride have helped foster a strong connection between the Slovenian people and the sport of cycling.

Roglič's success has also had economic benefits for Slovenian cycling. His popularity has attracted sponsors and investors who are eager to be associated with a global star. This influx of sponsorship money has been crucial in supporting the growth of cycling in Slovenia, providing funding for cycling teams, events, and youth programs. Roglič's presence has created a virtuous cycle where his success brings in more support, which in turn helps develop the next generation of cyclists.

Beyond the economic and infrastructural impact, Roglič's contribution to Slovenian cycling can also be seen in the way he inspires his fellow riders. Slovenian cyclists, whether they are professionals or amateurs, now look to Roglič as a source of motivation. His dedication to the sport and his ability to overcome adversity have become a model for others to follow. For

Slovenian cyclists who are just starting their careers, knowing that one of their own has reached the pinnacle of the sport gives them the belief that they too can succeed.

Roglič's influence has not only been felt in Slovenia but also in the broader cycling world. His success has helped shift attention to smaller cycling nations, proving that talent can emerge from anywhere, not just from traditional cycling powerhouses. This has inspired other countries with less-established cycling programs to invest more in the sport, recognizing that the next Roglič could come from anywhere.

The Evolution of Competitive Cycling Through Roglič's Eyes

Primož Roglič's career has spanned a transformative period in professional cycling, and through his experiences, we can trace the evolution of the sport over the past decade. From technological advancements to changes in race strategies and the increasing globalization of cycling, Roglič has witnessed and been part of these shifts. His perspective offers valuable insights into how the sport has changed and where it might be headed in the future.

One of the most significant changes Roglič has seen is the rise of technology in cycling. When he first began competing, the sport relied heavily on the rider's physical abilities and team strategies. While these elements are still crucial, modern cycling now incorporates advanced technology in nearly every aspect of training and competition. For instance, power meters, which measure a rider's output in real-time, have become standard tools for training and race preparation. Roglič, like many of his peers, has had to adapt to this new data-driven approach, where numbers and metrics guide much of the decision-making process.

In addition to power meters, advancements in bike design have also played a key role in the evolution of cycling. Bikes have become lighter, more aerodynamic, and equipped with cutting-edge materials designed to maximize performance. These improvements allow cyclists to go faster with less effort, leading to more competitive and exciting races. Roglič has spoken about how important it is for riders to stay informed about the latest technological developments, as even small improvements in equipment can make a significant difference in races.

However, Roglič has also highlighted that while technology has its benefits, it can sometimes take away from the human element of the sport. In interviews, he has expressed concern that cycling could become too focused on numbers and data, potentially overshadowing the instinctual and tactical aspects that make the sport exciting. Roglič believes that while technology should be embraced, it's important for riders to maintain a balance, relying on their experience and intuition just as much as on their gadgets.

Another major change Roglič has observed is the increasing internationalization of professional cycling. In the past, the sport was dominated by a handful of countries, with most of the top teams and riders coming from places like France, Italy, Spain, and Belgium. However, in recent years, cycling has become more global, with riders from countries all over the world competing at the highest levels. Roglič himself is a testament to this trend, as he hails from Slovenia, a country that wasn't traditionally known for producing top cyclists. This globalization has made the sport more diverse and competitive, with new talent emerging from unexpected places.

Roglič's career has also coincided with changes in race strategies. The traditional model, where teams would often rely on a single leader to win a race, has evolved. Modern teams are more flexible, with multiple riders capable of leading and winning stages. This shift has been driven partly by the increasing competitiveness of the peloton, as well as by the tactical complexities introduced by technology and data analysis. Roglič has thrived in this new environment, where riders need to be adaptable and able to seize opportunities as they arise.

The increasing speed of races is another evolution that Roglič has experienced firsthand. As training methods, nutrition, and equipment have improved, the overall pace of cycling races has increased. Today's riders are faster, stronger, and more efficient than ever before. Roglič has had to continually refine his training regimen to keep up with these demands, pushing his body to its limits to remain competitive. He has acknowledged that the sport has become more physically demanding over time, but he views this as a natural progression, where athletes are constantly pushing the boundaries of what is possible.

Roglič has also witnessed the growing importance of mental preparation in cycling. In the early days of his career, the focus was primarily on physical conditioning. However, as the sport has evolved, athletes have recognized the need for mental resilience and psychological training. Roglič, known for his calm demeanor and ability to stay focused under pressure, has spoken about the importance of mental toughness, particularly in high-stakes races like the Tour de France. He believes that cycling is as much a mental challenge as it is a physical one, and this aspect of the sport has become more pronounced as the competition has intensified.

Roglič has seen how the relationship between cyclists and fans has evolved. With the rise of social media, riders are now more accessible to their supporters than ever before. Roglič himself has embraced platforms like Instagram and Twitter, where he shares updates, interacts with fans, and gives them a glimpse into his life beyond cycling. This increased interaction has helped bridge the gap between athletes and their fans, making the sport more engaging and personal. Roglič believes that this connection with fans is essential for the future of cycling, as it helps build a loyal and passionate audience.

CONCLUSION

As we draw this biography of Primož Roglič to a close, we are reminded of the extraordinary journey of a man whose influence in the sport of cycling extends far beyond his victories on the podium. From the quiet hills of Slovenia to the most grueling climbs of the Grand Tours, Roglič's rise to the top of competitive cycling is a story of grit, adaptability, and the relentless pursuit of excellence.

Primož Roglič's career has been defined by challenges, both on and off the bike. From his early days as a ski jumper to his incredible transformation into one of the most dominant cyclists in the world, he has faced obstacles that would have deterred even the most talented athletes. But Roglič is no ordinary competitor—each setback has only served to deepen his resolve, sharpen his focus, and push him to new heights. Whether it was recovering from a devastating crash or finding the mental toughness to lead in some of the sport's most iconic races, Roglič has continually proven that resilience is his greatest asset.

But beyond the physical demands of cycling, Roglič's true legacy lies in his mental fortitude and strategic mastery. He is a rider who not only excels in individual time trials and mountainous stages but also understands the nuances of race strategy like few others. Roglič has redefined what it means to be a tactician in modern cycling—carefully managing his energy, biding his time, and executing his moves with precision. In a sport where a fraction of a second or a single miscalculation can determine the outcome, Roglič has earned a reputation as one of the most intelligent and calculated cyclists of his generation.

His story, however, is not just about individual accolades. Roglič's contribution to the sport goes far beyond his personal triumphs. As a leader, he has inspired his teammates, earning their respect through his work ethic, humility, and determination. His ability to push through pain and lead by example has made him a cornerstone of his team's success, particularly in the most prestigious races of the cycling calendar. Whether winning the Vuelta a España or battling for the yellow jersey in the Tour de France, Roglič's presence on a team has always been invaluable, both for his leadership and his ability to deliver when it matters most.

Roglič's career is also an attestation to the idea that success is not achieved overnight. His path to stardom was unconventional, beginning with a sport far removed from cycling. Yet, his transition from ski jumping to cycling underscores the power of reinvention and the belief that one's journey is never set in stone. Roglič's story serves as an inspiration to all athletes and dreamers, reminding us that with enough determination and willingness to adapt, we can achieve greatness in areas we might never have imagined.

The highs and lows of his career—his dramatic comebacks, heartbreaking near-misses, and brilliant victories—are all part of a narrative that transcends the sport itself. Roglič's journey resonates with fans and fellow athletes not just because of his success, but because of how he has handled every situation with grace and unshakable determination. Whether celebrating his hard-earned victories or facing moments of profound disappointment, Roglič has always maintained the composure and character that mark him as a true champion.

As Primož Roglič continues to race toward new challenges, his legacy in the world of cycling is already secure. He has left an indelible mark on the sport—shaping it not just through his dominance in time trials and mountain stages, but by setting a standard of professionalism, humility, and resilience that others will strive to follow.

His story is one of transformation, perseverance, and the power of belief in oneself, reminding us all that greatness is not just about winning, but about how we face adversity and rise above it.

The legacy of Primož Roglič will endure long after his time in the saddle comes to an end. He has shown that even in the world of professional cycling, where the margins for success are razor-thin, there is always room for reinvention, innovation, and heart. His career is a blueprint for how to navigate the challenges of elite competition with grace and resolve, and his journey will continue to inspire cyclists and fans alike for years to come.

This is the enduring legacy of Primož Roglič: a rider who not only mastered the dynamics of speed and strategy but also redefined what it means to succeed through resilience, intelligence, and an unwavering commitment to his craft. His story is one that will be remembered not just for the races he won, but for the champion he became.

Printed in Great Britain
by Amazon